ENERGY
Now and in
the Future

Wind Power

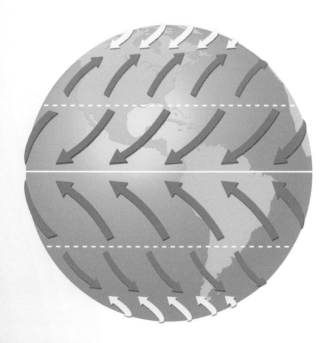

Neil Morris

A⁺
Smart Apple Media

Smart Apple Media
P.O. Box 3263
Mankato, MN 56002

Printed in the United States of America

Library of Congress Cataloging-in-Publication Data

Morris, Neil, 1946-
  Wind power / by Neil Morris.
     p. cm. -- (Energy now and in the future)
  Includes bibliographical references and index.
  Summary: "Discusses how different types of turbines can be used to harness wind power to make electricity, the advantages and disadvantages of wind power, and ways wind power could be used in the future"--Provided by publisher.
  ISBN 978-1-59920-344-7 (hardcover)
  1. Wind power--Juvenile literature. I. Title.
  TJ820.M68 2010
  333.9'2--dc22

                                                                2008043227

Designed by Helen James
Edited by Mary-Jane Wilkins
Artwork by Guy Callaby
Picture research by Su Alexander

Photograph acknowledgements
Page 8 Ashley Cooper/Corbis; 10 Frans Lemmens/Zefa/Corbis; 11 Richard T Nowitz/Corbis; 12 Macduff Everton/Corbis; 15 Tom Bean/Corbis; 17 Copyright The Poul La Cour Museum, Askov,Denmark; 20 Ingo Wagner/epa/Corbis; 21 Anthony West/Corbis; 22 Chinch Gryniewicz; Ecoscene/Corbis; 23 Lowell Georgia/Corbis; Murat Taner/Zefa/Corbis; 27 Ingo Wagner/DPA/Corbis; 29 Siemens Press Picture; 31 Gideon Mendel/Corbis; 32 Julia Waterlow; Eye Ubiquitous/Corbis; 33 Kerstin Geier; Gallo Images/Corbis; 36 Mast Irham/epa/Corbis; 37 Jim Sugar/Corbis; 38 Naturfoto Honal/Corbis; 40 Copyright SkySails; 43 Ben Shepard copyright Project Web
Front cover Penny Tweedie/Corbis

9 8 7 6 5 4 3 2 1

Contents

Harnessing the Power of the Wind

Wind is a valuable source of energy. People have used the wind for centuries to drive mills and pumps. More recently, wind is used to power modern turbines. Wind is a renewable resource—it will never run out. We can harness it to produce electricity. Wind power has become increasingly important in the twenty-first century.

Wind is air on the move. It is caused by the Sun, which is the original source of all the world's energy. Solar heat warms some parts of Earth more than other parts, and this affects the blanket of air that surrounds our planet. For example, land areas heat up more quickly than the sea, but they also cool down more quickly. As air becomes warmer, it expands and rises. Cooler air then flows in to replace the warm air, in a process called circulation.

Winds of the World

There is a pattern to the world's wind circulation. The land and sea are hottest in the tropical region near the equator. Warm air rises and cooler air moves in to replace it. This movement of air creates the trade winds, which take their name from the fact that they once powered merchant sailing ships. The trade winds usually blow from east to west because of the rotation of Earth, which deflects them.

Further away from the equator, there are bands of westerly winds caused by surface air reaching an area that spins more slowly (because its circumference

Land and Sea Breezes

Why is it usually breezy at the coast? During the day, the land is warmer so air rises above it. Cooler air comes off the sea to replace it, causing an onshore sea breeze. At night, the land cools faster than the sea, and air generally flows off the land, creating an offshore land breeze. This small repeating pattern of air circulation is a good example of how winds form.

The Coriolis Effect

In 1835, French scientist Gaspard-Gustave de Coriolis (1792–1843) described the effect that was later named after him. Coriolis noticed that Earth's rotation affects the motion of anything traveling across Earth's surface—including moving air. Winds moving away from the equator curve to the east. Those moving toward the equator curve west.

is smaller). In the area near the poles, cool air reaches faster-spinning areas and forms easterly winds.

Can We Rely on the Wind?

In general terms, we can rely on the wind continuing to blow. The global pattern of wind circulation is caused by energy from the Sun, which experts say will shine for another 5 billion years. There is no reason to believe that Earth will not continue to rotate, adding to the creation of wind through the Coriolis effect. However, local winds in any one spot on Earth can vary, and this has led some critics to claim that wind power is unreliable. Local research gives planners a great deal of information about average wind conditions and helps them plan accordingly.

Polar easterlies

Westerlies

30º North

Trade winds

Equator

Trade winds

30º South

Westerlies

Polar easterlies

The global pattern of wind circulation is caused by temperature differences and Earth's rotation. Moving air is cooler the further it is from the equator.

Wind Strength

We measure the strength of the wind according to the speed of the moving air. Wind speed is given in miles (km) per hour or feet (m) per second. Meteorologists keep records of wind speed, along with other data. This gives energy specialists information to work with when positioning turbines.

The two most important factors are the average wind speed and wind distribution. These indicate how windy a particular place is. The distribution explains variations in the general pattern of wind speed in one place. This is called the Weibull distribution. It is named after Swedish scientist Wallodi Weibull (1887–1979), who first described it. The diagram opposite is a good example. The average wind speed in this place was worked out from measurements taken over a year.

The winds off the sea in Morecambe Bay, in northwest England, have bent these trees into dramatic shapes.

Useful Wind

Because of the design of spinning blades, very low and very high wind speeds cannot generate power. Very strong winds turn the blades too fast, making the turbine structure dangerous. Modern windmills have control systems (see page 21). Turbines start and stop turning at specific wind speeds. These usually vary between 10–82 feet (3–25 m) per second (levels 2–9 on the Beaufort scale). The maximum useful wind speed is generally about 49 feet (15 m) per second (Beaufort 7).

These were plotted on a graph, which shows that the median (or middle value) is 6.6 meters (21.6 ft) per second. The graph also shows that the wind speed was often half that level, but rarely double that amount.

WEIBULL DISTRIBUTION OF WIND SPEED

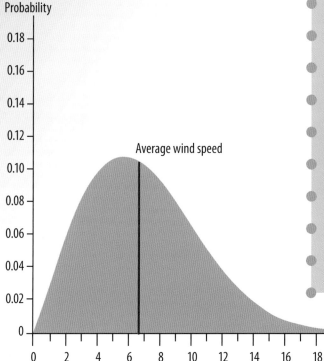

Beaufort Scale

Weather forecasts today still give wind speeds according to a scale developed in 1805 by Francis Beaufort (1774–1857), who was an officer in the British Royal Navy.

Beaufort number	Description	miles (km) per hour	
0	Calm	<1	(<1)
1	Light air	1–3	(1–5)
2	Light breeze	4–7	(6–11)
3	Gentle breeze	8–12	(12–19)
4	Moderate breeze	13–18	(20–28)
5	Fresh breeze	19–24	(29–38)
6	Strong breeze	25–31	(39–49)
7	Moderate gale	32–38	(50–61)
8	Fresh gale	39–46	(62–74)
9	Strong gale	47–54	(75–88)
10	Whole gale	55–63	(89–102)
11	Storm	64–72	(103–118)
12	Hurricane	73+	(119+)

How Do We Measure Wind Speed?

Today, wind speed is usually measured with a device called an anemometer (from the Greek word *anemos*, meaning wind). The first wind meter was invented in Italy around 1450 and was based on a spinning disc. In 1846, Irish physicist Thomas Robinson (1792–1882) invented a four-cup anemometer. This device had cups that caught wind from any direction and turned. The wind speed was measured by the number of turns the cups made in a given period and was registered on a set of dials. Today, most anemometers have three cups, and there are also smaller, handheld versions with built-in rotating propellers. The highest wind speeds—caused by tornadoes—are measured by Doppler radar. In 1999, this system measured a world record wind speed of 318 miles (512 km) per hour in a tornado that devastated Oklahoma City.

From Sailing Ships to Windmills

Humans probably first harnessed the power of the wind to use sails to move boats across water. Early rafts may have had sails attached, but archaeological evidence for this is difficult to find. The earliest historical information records sailing boats more than 5,000 years ago in ancient Egypt.

Against the Current

Ancient Egyptians made their first boats from bundles of papyrus reeds lashed together. By 3000 B.C., the boats had oars and a long, narrow sail. The center of Egyptian society was the Nile River, which formed the main highway of the empire. The Egyptians used boats to fish, hunt, and transport grain and cattle. Sailors traveled downstream toward the Mediterranean Sea on the strong current of the Nile. They used wind power to travel upstream and return south to Thebes, Aswan, and beyond.

Trading Ships

During the Egyptian Old Kingdom (2686–2181 B.C.), shipbuilders made stronger vessels of wooden planks. These sturdy ships could venture farther from land. Egyptian sailors first made their way to the Mediterranean island

Traditional Egyptian boats called feluccas still sail on the Nile today. They remind us that sailors have used the power of the wind since ancient times.

of Crete (the home of the Minoan civilization). They also sailed to Phoenicia (modern Syria, Lebanon, and Israel), where they acquired the famous trees called cedars of Lebanon. By the time of the Middle Kingdom (2055–1650 B.C.), there was regular sea trade between the two empires. The Egyptians then looked toward East Africa and the Indian Ocean. They carried boats in pieces across the eastern desert to the Red Sea, where they put them together again. According to the ancient Greek historian Herodotus, around 600 B.C. an Egyptian trading fleet left a Red Sea port and returned to Egypt more than two years later via the Mediterranean.

Powering Across the Oceans

Sailing ships were used by early explorers and adventurers. Between the ninth and twelfth centuries, Vikings made the strongest, fastest ships. On the open sea, their longships were powered by a single square sail. This was made of tough woolen cloth strengthened by strips of leather. In the tenth century, the Norwegian Viking Erik the Red sailed across the Atlantic Ocean to Greenland. His son, Leif Eriksson, traveled even farther, to the coast of North America, around the year 1000—nearly 500 years before the transatlantic voyages of Christopher Columbus.

This ninth-century Viking ship was powered by oars and a large square sail.

Speeding with the Wind

Fast sailing ships are still used for sport and recreation. In the nineteenth century, before airplanes, clipper ships were the fastest type of transportation in the world. They were also faster than the first successful steamship that was launched in 1807. Clipper ships may have been named for their sharp bows, fast clipping speed, or because they clipped days off sailing times. Clippers had light wooden hulls and up to six rows of sails on at least three masts. They carried tea from China to Europe, wool from Australia, and people around the Americas during the California gold rush. Clippers reached speeds up to 25 miles (41 km) per hour (22 knots).

This old post mill stands on the Swedish island of Öland. There are hundreds of windmills on the island. Some date back to the seventeenth century.

Wind-Powered Wheels

The first person known to have used a wind-powered wheel was the Greek scientist and inventor Hero. He lived in the Roman-controlled Egyptian city of Alexandria around A.D. 10–70. Hero invented an organ played by the wind. The wind turned the sails of a wheel, pushing a piston pump that forced air through the organ pipes.

By the seventh century, the first windmills were being constructed in Persia (modern-day Iran). These mills ground (or milled) grain such as wheat. The mill wheels and sails were parallel to the ground and turned on a vertical shaft that came out of a square tower. The design was probably based on early waterwheels, which had been used for many centuries. As the wind caught the sails and turned the horizontal wheel, the attached shaft turned a pair of stones. Grain poured between the stones was ground into flour.

Spreading Technology

The new technology spread east in the 1220s, when the forces of the great Mongol conqueror Genghis Khan captured Persian millwrights and took them to China. By that time, windmills had also spread to Europe, possibly introduced by Crusaders returning from

Does the Old Technology Still Work?

The technology still works, but millers find that wind is less efficient and powerful than other sources of energy. James Watt (1736–1819) built the first steam-powered flour mill in 1780. In the twentieth century, steam was overtaken by electricity. Today, flour is usually milled between electrically powered steel rollers rather than stones. Nevertheless, some old windmills have been renovated and still produce stone-ground flour. Outwood post mill, in Surrey, England, was built in 1665 and is the oldest working windmill in the United Kingdom.

the wars in the Middle East. By the late twelfth century, European millwrights had begun to set their wind-powered wheels in the vertical position that is used today. They found their windmills were more powerful when the wheel turned on a horizontal shaft. Windmills were especially popular in parts of Europe where there were few fast-flowing streams to drive watermills.

Post Mills

Early European windmills had a box-like wooden body that contained the millstones and other machinery, such as gears. The box was mounted on a large wooden post attached to the horizontal windshaft (or axle). The vertical sails were outside the box, attached to the windshaft. The entire post mill structure could be turned to face and catch the wind, whichever direction it was blowing from. Workers pushed the post mill around when the wind changed.

Turning Towers

The next windmill development took place in the fifteenth century, when all the machinery was put inside a fixed tower with a revolving cap on top. The sails were attached to the cap so that they could more easily turn to face the wind. Wooden versions were called smock mills, and the sturdier stone or brick versions are known as tower mills. From that time, tower mills became common throughout Europe.

This diagram of a tower mill shows the working parts, stores and accommodation. Grain was poured on to the millstones to make meal (coarse flour).

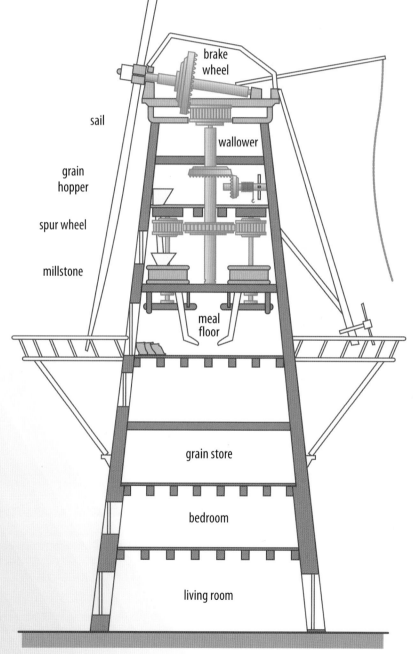

brake wheel

sail

wallower

grain hopper

spur wheel

millstone

meal floor

grain store

bedroom

living room

WIND POWER

Windshaft, Gears, and Cogs

Most windmills have four sails that drive a windshaft. A toothed cogwheel attached to the windshaft turns another wheel linked to a vertical main shaft. This shaft turns grooved millstones, and grain is poured into holes in the stones to be ground into flour. The action of the linked cogwheels turns the millstones about five times faster than the wind-driven sails.

Draining and Raising Water

The Netherlands is famous for windmills, but many of them are not mills at all. They should really be called wind pumps, because they are used to move water. Dutch people have been using wind power to drain their land since the fifteenth century. Almost half of the land is below sea level. Much of this land has been reclaimed from the sea by pumping water into drainage channels and building banks and dikes around areas of land called polders. The pumps used the same system as mills, turning a scoop wheel instead of millstones. The turning wheel scooped up water and poured it into a higher-level ditch or basin. Engineers often built several wind pumps in a row so that water could be raised slightly higher by each one. In the nineteenth century, there were 9,000 windmills and wind pumps in the Netherlands, but many were replaced by steam engines.

A series of three wind pumps reclaims land by moving water from the polder to a drainage channel. This channel takes the water back to the sea.

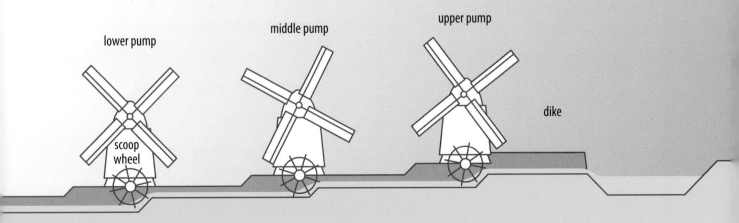

lower pump

middle pump

upper pump

dike

scoop wheel

polder water | lower basin | intermediate basin | waterway across dike | drainage channel

Pumping Up

In southern Europe, which has a warm Mediterranean climate, wind pumps traditionally were used to bring water to the surface from deep underground. On the Greek island of Crete, there were once 10,000 white-sailed pumps. Today, most have been replaced by electric and diesel-driven engines.

During the last two centuries, small wind pumps have been used in the United States. The turning shaft drives a pump rod that operates a piston to pump water to the surface. A relatively small wind-powered pump can pump about 53 gallons (200 L) of water a minute from a depth of about 100 feet (30 m). The water is stored in a tank and used to irrigate crops or as drinking water.

This wind pump provides water for cattle on a farm in Nebraska.

Wind-Powered Pumps Today

Wind pumps are still used all over the world, especially in dry areas. Concerns about the environment and a desire to use renewable sources of energy have increased interest in this traditional technology. Some wind-powered pumps still exist in the United States and Australia, and manufacturers are promoting their environmental advantages. Wind pumps are particularly useful in the arid regions of Africa, such as Kenya, Namibia, and South Africa, where they provide water for villagers and livestock.

Sawmill

In 1592, Dutch millwright Cornelis Corneliszoon (1550–1607) invented a wind-driven sawmill. He fixed the main shaft of the mill to saw blades that moved up and down. The blades cut lengths of timber as they passed through—up to 30 times faster than men. The mill was mounted on a raft so it could be turned into the wind.

Wind-Powered Electricity

Charles Brush (1849–1929) was an American inventor best known for his arc lamp. This was an important form of electric lighting before the invention of the incandescent light bulb. In 1879, Brush devised an electric lighting system for a public square in Cleveland, Ohio. Brush's arc lamps were soon lighting streets in Boston, New York, and San Francisco and making their inventor rich. In 1888, Brush decided to try a new system for generating electricity. He had been using a horse-drawn treadmill to power a dynamo, or simple generator, but then he replaced horse power with the wind. Brush built a large windwheel in the garden of his Cleveland mansion. The wheel drove a dynamo that charged 408 batteries in the basement of the mansion. These powered 350 incandescent lights and some of his own arc lamps.

Brush's Wind-Dynamo Facts and Figures

Tower height: 60 feet (18 m)

Tower weight: 40 tons (36 t)

Wheel diameter: 56 feet (17 m)

Number of wooden wheel blades: 144

Wind shaft length: 20 feet (6 m)

Fantail length: 60 feet (18 m)

Top wheel speed: 10 revolutions per minute

Electricity production: 12 kW

Increasing Efficiency

In 1890, Poul la Cour (1846–1908), a Danish high school teacher, scientist, and inventor, began testing ways of using windwheels to generate electricity. La Cour was particularly interested in supplying electric power—which all scientists saw as the future—to small villages in the

Poul la Cour's early wind turbine was built along the lines of a traditional windmill. Later versions had an iron framework and four sails.

countryside. He built a wind turbine that was based on traditional windmills, with six sails mounted on a wooden tower. The wheels were attached to turbine buildings. La Cour found that turbines that turned faster and had fewer rotor blades were more efficient for producing electricity. Denmark has remained one of the world's largest producers of wind energy.

Scientific Progress over a Century

Charles Brush and Poul la Cour were pioneers in the field of wind-generated electricity. La Cour founded the Society of Wind Electricians in Denmark in 1903. The following year, he published the world's first journal on the subject of wind-generated electricity. Some environmentalists believe that more research could lead to the development of more effective technology.

The World Wind Energy Association (WWEA) was founded in 2001, with headquarters in Bonn, Germany. The association holds an annual global conference in a different part of the world each year. Since 2007, the WWEA has been represented on the Economic and Social Council of the United Nations. Perhaps we should put even more effort into scientific progress?

Turbines Today

The most important way we use wind power today is in generating electricity. Today's wind turbines have an electric generator in their housing, unlike those developed at the end of the nineteenth century. They are sometimes called aerogenerators (*aero* meaning air or wind).

Electricity generation began during the nineteenth century. In 1831, British scientist Michael Faraday (1791–1867) discovered that he could create electricity by moving a magnet through a coil of copper wire. This process is called electromagnetic induction. It led to the invention of the electric generator, which works by changing mechanical energy into electrical energy. The power of moving air provides the mechanical energy for wind turbines by turning the rotor blades. The blades are connected to a shaft, which is also attached to a generator. Inside the generator, the shaft makes magnets spin inside wire coils to produce electricity.

The Rotor

The rotor is the assembly of blades that is turned by the wind. The blades are made of strong polyester plastic reinforced with glass fiber or carbon fiber and attached to a steel hub. The blades look like an airplane wing or airfoil. The upper side facing the wind is curved, and the lower side is flat. This creates greater air pressure on the lower side, giving lift and forcing the blade forward so the hub rotates. Large turbines have an automatic controlling device to change the pitch (or angle) of the blades. If the wind is too strong and the blades are moving too fast, the blade is turned slightly to reduce the lift and speed.

Horizontal Axis Turbines

There are two basic types of wind turbines: horizontal axis wind turbines (HAWT) and vertical axis wind turbines (VAWT). The most common type today is the three-blade HAWT (see opposite). This has proved to be the most efficient for wind turbines with rotor diameters of 130–295 feet (40–90 m). The three blades make the rotation smoother and the turbine seems less visibly intrusive than two, four, or more blades.

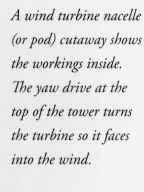

A wind turbine nacelle (or pod) cutaway shows the workings inside. The yaw drive at the top of the tower turns the turbine so it faces into the wind.

Are Wind Turbines Noisy?

Most experts agree that modern turbines produce less mechanical noise than early versions, although the flow of air over the blades still makes a whooshing sound. The UK Sustainable Development Commission says: "Turbine design has improved substantially as the technology has advanced, with noise from the moving parts progressively reduced. The public's concern about noise from turbines is often related to perceptions rather than actual experience. Detailed studies have shown that the very low levels of low frequency noise from wind turbines will not normally cause adverse health effects." The commission says the sound from a turbine is about 90–100 dB, which is similar to a pneumatic drill at a distance of 23 feet (7 m); or 50–60 dB at 130 feet (40 m), which is similar to a busy office; or 25–35 dB at 1,640 feet (500 m), which is similar to a quiet room. The noise is an issue only if you are very close to a turbine.

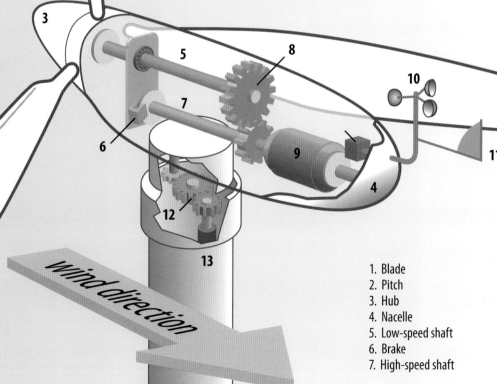

wind direction

1. Blade
2. Pitch
3. Hub
4. Nacelle
5. Low-speed shaft
6. Brake
7. High-speed shaft
8. Gear
9. Generator
10. Anemometer
11. Wind vane
12. Yaw drive
13. Tower

Tower and Pod

Towers are usually made of steel or concrete. The tallest reach well over 330 feet (100 m). One of the latest German wind turbines is 443 feet (135 m) high at the hub and has a rotor diameter of 413 feet (126 m). Manufacturers prefabricate the towers in three or four parts and use cranes to assemble and erect them at the site.

Taller towers have less turbulence from ground features and catch the wind better. At the top of the tower, the streamlined nacelle (or pod) turns according to the wind direction. A wind vane at the back of the pod sends signals to an onboard computer that calculates the best direction and moves the pod with an electric yaw motor.

Gearing Up

Inside the pod, the turning shaft is connected to a gearbox. This has a set of gears (or toothed wheels) that increase the spinning speed. The gearbox converts the energy from the rotor. When the rotor is turning

Opposite: Towers are hollow so that engineers can climb a ladder inside to check and service working parts.

Assembly workers are dwarfed by the giant nacelle of this German wind turbine. One of three rotor blades has been installed on the hub, at a height of 407 feet (124 m).

Withstanding the Weather

Manufacturers have to allow for extreme weather conditions when designing and building wind turbines. The tower has to withstand very strong forces and is built on sturdy foundations. Some manufacturers offer what they call "hurricane-resistant" towers. Most turbines have automatic braking systems that slow the speed of the shaft if it is turning dangerously fast. They often have a mechanical disc brake behind the hub, which backs up the actions of the pitched blades and can be used as a parking brake when the turbine is out of action.

To counteract lightning strikes during thunderstorms, turbines have special receptors that conduct electricity to the ground. These include aluminum blade tips, metal discs along the blades, and conductors along the pod and tower. The lightning is kept away from sensitive parts of the turbine that might be damaged. In case of fire, turbines also have automatic extinguishers. Many turbines have heating and cooling systems for the working parts, which are especially useful in extreme climates.

at 10–22 rpm, it converts that to about 1,500 rpm, so the generator shaft is turned much more quickly and produces electricity more effectively.

Do Wind Turbines Work Most of the Time?

Turbines rely on wind conditions. Opponents to wind power say that turbines are inefficient and work only 30 percent of the time. Industry experts claim that is the overall percentage of electricity they produce compared with the maximum electricity they could generate in theory. Modern wind turbines produce electricity 70–85 percent of the time, but at different rates depending on wind speed. Over the course of a year, they generate between 25 and 40 percent of their possible maximum output (with usually more in winter than summer). This compares with biomass plants at 60–90 percent, combined cycle gas turbine (CCGT) plants at 70–85 percent, coal-fired and nuclear plants at 65–85 percent, and hydropower at 25–50 percent.

Vertical Axis Turbines

Vertical axis wind turbines (VAWTs) have a windshaft or main axle that stands upright from the ground (like the tower of a HAWT). The turbine blades do not swivel to face the wind. They are pushed by winds from any direction. This design allows the generator to be close to the ground, which makes it easier to reach for servicing and repairs. However, ground winds tend to be more turbulent than high-level winds.

Different Designs

In 1931, French aeronautical engineer Georges Darrieus (1888–1979) patented his vertical turbine. It was a distinctive shape, with up to four curved blades attached to a vertical shaft. It was soon known as the eggbeater. This is the only VAWT that has been made commercially in any volume, but it does have problems. It does not perform well in high winds and has to be held firmly in place with steel cables or an outer structure. Another issue is that the eggbeater is difficult to start in normal winds, so an electric motor kick-starts its rotation.

Georges Darrieus's turbine patent covered almost any arrangement of vertical airfoil blades. This made designs difficult for other engineers. One later design was the giromill (or H-bar or crossarm design), which has straight vertical blades attached to a central tower with horizontal supports. The giromill design is simpler to build than the eggbeater, but the

This vertical axis turbine can produce 130 kW of electricity. The E-112 shown on page 20 can generate 6 MW, which is 46 times greater.

How Efficient?

Experts have found that vertical turbines generally are not as efficient as horizontal turbines. Most VAWTs produce energy at only half the efficiency of HAWTs. This is mainly due to the additional drag they are exposed to as their blades turn back into the wind on the way back to their starting point.

Investing in Wind Power

Engineers such as Georges Darrieus invented new turbines 80 years ago, and inventors are still working on innovative designs. Some environmental groups think we should invest much more money in turbine research and development—in the hope that engineers may be able to increase their efficiency. Others feel that governments should be investing more in wind power so that the initial costs can be subsidized and companies are encouraged to develop new systems. Large wind turbines are expensive to develop and build, but once they are running, the power needed to run them—the wind—is free. Some countries have what is called a feed-in tariff. This is the price per unit of electricity that a national or regional energy supplier pays for electricity from renewable sources (including wind) from private generators. The government regulates the tariff (or price). This helps new energy-generating companies to become established so they can compete with older suppliers that mainly burn fossil fuels.

structure is heavier and the blades need to be much stronger. A similar version is called a cycloturbine.

This series of Darrieus eggbeater turbines stretches across a hillside in California.

Onshore and Offshore

Individual wind turbines do not produce enormous amounts of electricity compared with power stations fired by fossil fuels. A large aerogenerator may produce just 1 megawatt (MW) of power, though the largest are six or seven times more powerful. If you compare this with a large coal-fired power station, which can produce 5,000 MW, it is easy to see why energy companies put wind turbines together in large groups.

Groups called wind farms (or sometimes wind parks) form small power plants. They are often positioned on land, but there is increasing interest in offshore wind farms.

According to the World Wind Energy Association (WWEA), wind is used to generate electricity in more than 70 countries. The amount of electricity produced has been growing by more than 25 percent a year in recent times. In 2007, wind generated 1.3 percent of the electricity used in the world and provided electricity for more than 25 million

PRODUCTION OF WIND POWER (MW)

AND PERCENTAGE OF WORLD OUTPUT (%)

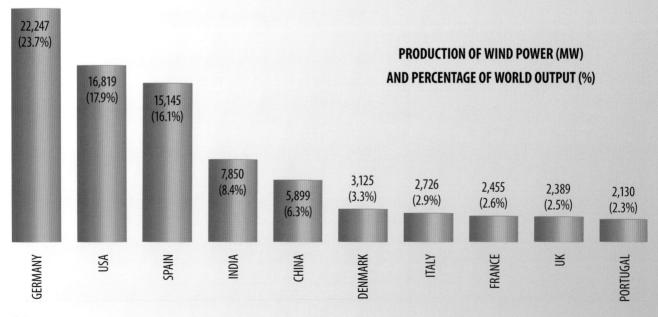

22,247 (23.7%)	16,819 (17.9%)	15,145 (16.1%)	7,850 (8.4%)	5,899 (6.3%)	3,125 (3.3%)	2,726 (2.9%)	2,455 (2.6%)	2,389 (2.5%)	2,130 (2.3%)
GERMANY	USA	SPAIN	INDIA	CHINA	DENMARK	ITALY	FRANCE	UK	PORTUGAL

This wind farm has been built on top of a hill. This is a good location for wind power.

homes. In some countries, wind-generated electricity adds up to more than 40 percent. As the table (opposite) shows, the four leading wind-energy countries make up two-thirds of the world's production.

Finding the Right Location

Engineers look for the best sites for wind farms. They study local winds in likely locations for many months and make wind maps for energy companies to study. Experts have found that long narrow hilltops are good sites. These winds can be more powerful as they move up a hill and accelerate over the top of the hill, adding wind speed to generate more energy.

What Is a Watt?

A watt (W) is a unit of power that measures the rate of producing or using energy. The term was named after Scottish engineer James Watt (1736–1819), who developed an improved steam engine. Watt measured his engine's performance in horsepower (hp). One horsepower equals 746 watts. Today, watts are generally used to measure electric power.

1 kilowatt (kW) = 1 thousand watts
1 megawatt (MW) = 1 million watts
1 gigawatt (GW) = 1 billion watts

What Are the Advantages of Wind Power?

The main advantage is that wind is a simple form of renewable energy (see page 34). What else could you add? The Global Wind Energy Council lists 12 advantages:

"Wind power. . .

• is clean, free, and indigenous;

• combats climate change;

• reduces air pollution;

• provides energy security;

• diversifies energy supply;

• eliminates imported fuels;

• prevents conflict over natural resources;

• improves rural electrification and reduces poverty;

• creates jobs, regional growth, and innovation;

• hedges price volatility of fossil fuels;

• delivers power on a large scale;

• is modular and quick to install."

Winds are usually stronger near the coast, so many wind farms are located at nearshore sites. These are either on land within 2 miles (3 km) of the coast or at sea within 6 miles (10 km) of the coast. In this 8 mile (13 km) wide zone, wind farms can use both onshore and offshore winds.

Largest Wind Farm

Horse Hollow Wind Center is the world's largest wind farm. It is near Abilene, Texas, and 300 miles (500 km) from the nearest coast on the Gulf of Mexico. The center was built in 2005–06 and produces enough electricity to power about 220,000 homes. When the wind farm opened, some local people complained about the appearance of the turbines and the noise they created. The case went to court, but a judge and jury decided that the wind farm was not a nuisance and did not invade the locals' privacy.

Horse Hollow Center Facts and Figures

Total area: 93 square miles (240 sq km)

Number of turbines: 421

Turbine height: 262 feet (80 m)

Cutoff wind speed: 56 miles (90 km) per hour (Beaufort 10)

Total electricity production: 735 MW

Farming Ocean Winds

The surface of the ocean is much smoother than land, so the average wind speed over open water is usually much higher. This means that offshore wind farms can be more efficient and powerful than onshore farms. Turbines are easiest to build in shallow waters, because their

foundations have to be built on the seabed. Countries with long coastlines and shallow continental shelves—such as Denmark and the UK—offer many good locations for offshore wind farms.

This row of nearshore turbines is just off the coast of Denmark.

Success at Sea

The Horns Rev wind farm, 9 miles (14 km) off the Danish coast in the North Sea, was built in 2002. It has 80 turbines, each 230 feet (70 m tall), and covers a 215 square foot (20 sq km) area of sea. The turbines are set 1,840 feet (560 m) in a maximum water depth of 125 feet (38 m). The farm's operators claim the offshore farm produces twice the electricity as a similar onshore wind farm.

Can Turbines Be Close Together?

They can be fairly close together. However, each wind turbine creates turbulence, spoiling the powerful flow of air to other turbines by creating gusts. Engineers work out exactly how to position a series of turbines. They are often spaced three to five rotor diameters apart at right angles to the direction of the prevailing wind. If there is another row of turbines, they are positioned between five and ten rotor diameters away. The precise positioning can make a huge difference to the overall efficiency of a wind farm.

WIND POWER

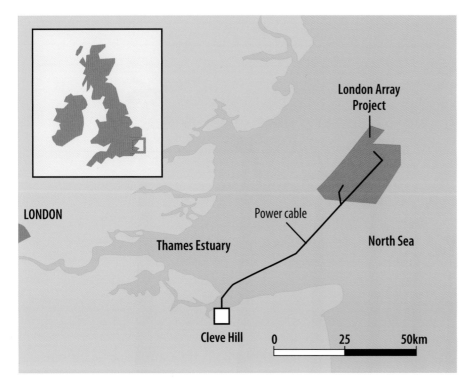

London Array
Project

Power cable

LONDON

Thames Estuary

North Sea

Cleve Hill

0   25   50km

The London Array wind farm could be completed by 2010. The turbines will stand in water up to 75 feet (23 m) deep and will be up to 328 feet (100 m) tall. Generated electricity will be fed into the British national grid at Cleve Hill.

Biggest in the World

At the end of 2006, approval was given for the construction of the world's largest offshore wind farm—London Array (an array is a very large group). It will be built on and between two sandbanks more than 12 miles (20 km) off the Kent and Essex coasts, in the outer Thames estuary. It will take four years to build and will produce enough electricity to power about 750,000 homes. The government hopes that the array will produce 10 percent of its renewable energy target when it comes into operation.

London Array Facts and Figures

Total area: 95 square miles (245 sq km)

Number of turbines: 341

Turbine height: 328 feet (100 m)

Cut-off wind speed: 56 miles (90 km) per hour (Beaufort 10)

Total electricity production: up to 1 GW

A Supergrid under the Sea

The electricity generated by wind turbines is fed into cables that join the main electricity network at the nearest available point. Offshore wind farm cables run beneath the surface of the sea, usually on the seabed. In Europe, Irish and Swiss engineers are working on a project called a subsea supergrid. The idea is to connect many small electricity networks from offshore wind farms along Europe's coastline. When the wind blows over a farm on the supergrid, its cables will carry electricity

A 170 foot (52 m) rotor blade is carefully checked at a factory in Denmark. It has been made in one piece, and its curved shape must be exactly right.

to where it is needed most. If the wind is not blowing over the North Sea, it may be windy in the Baltic or Irish Sea. The aim of the supergrid is to make wind power more accessible and reliable, while at the same time linking separate countries so that they can trade energy.

Onshore or Offshore?

This is a difficult question. Offshore turbines cause some problems for ships, but energy companies and environmentalists are generally in favor of them. One proposed offshore project is in Nantucket Sound, a large area of shallow water off the coast of Massachusetts. The environmental group Greenpeace says: "This wind farm project will provide 74 percent of Cape Cod's energy needs with clean and safe wind power. It could dramatically reduce the need for the Cape's current oil and gas burning power plant, which caused a major oil spill in Buzzard's Bay in 2003. . . Greenpeace has 30 years history defending the world's oceans. We would. . . oppose this proposal if we felt that it posed long-term threats to the marine ecosystem of Nantucket Sound. We agree Nantucket Sound is a beautiful place that is heavily used by tourists, locals, part-time residents, fisherpeople, and commercial interests. We support offshore wind in Nantucket Sound because we see it as an important step in our fight for renewable energy solutions to global warming."

Small-Scale Turbines

Small-scale wind power can supply individual homes, businesses, or small communities. In the industrialized world, this is a popular way for environmentally conscious people to produce their own electricity. One of the most successful markets for "small wind" is the United States. The American Wind Energy Association (AWEA) claims that energy generated by small turbines (up to 100 kW capacity) is growing by 18–20 percent every year.

Encouraging Wind Power

Wind systems are expensive to install, and the initial cost may take more than five years to pay off in reduced electricity bills for a homeowner. In many countries, the government offers grants toward the cost of installing a small turbine. Many governments allow homeowners to sell surplus electricity created by the turbine to the national power grid. This seems fair and increases the overall percentage of electricity produced from renewable sources.

Micro Turbines

Some very small (or micro) turbines supply energy for battery-charging systems. These are often used on boats and for some homes. For houses, there are two kinds of turbines. One is mounted on a mast and stands on

Ecovillages for the Future?

Ecovillages are communities in which people try to live in a way that does as little harm as possible to the natural environment. Ecovillagers do all they can to keep their soil, water, and air clean, and they prefer to use renewable energy. Many rely on the wind (and solar power) for electricity, because they consider these to be the most environmentally friendly methods. These examples of modern living could encourage others to follow the trend.

the ground near the building. The other is the less expensive roof-mounted turbine, which is often attached to a chimney. People considering their own wind system need to know the average wind speed and direction where they live and get expert advice before they install a system.

People living in an ecovillage in Scotland use electricity supplied by a wind turbine.

Problems with Small Wind

Some reports have found that rooftop turbines produce only about a quarter of an average household's electricity needs, which has disappointed some householders. Small turbines do not always work well in urban areas, where wind often blows in gusts. Some have found that roof-mounted turbines cause structural damage to chimneys and gable ends. Turbulence also puts great stress on the turbines and shortens their life, though most experts say that they should last up to 20 years. People may notice vibration and noise from the turbine. As with other technologies, increased use and technical developments may eradicate these problems and make home installation more attractive in the near future.

WIND POWER

Off-Grid in China

China is a vast country with an enormous population (the world's largest) and fast-growing energy needs. Other countries supply China with renewable technology, including wind turbines. By the end of 2005, China had 59 wind farms with 1,854 turbines. The country was tenth in the world for wind-generated electricity. Two years later, it was fifth (see page 24).

By 2020, the Chinese government plans to generate 30 GW of wind power—five times more than in 2007. Much of this will come from small, off-grid projects in remote communities. One of the most successful small-scale wind energy programs is in the northern region of Inner Mongolia. Approximately 130,000 small turbines provide electricity for more than half a million people.

Practical Action in Sri Lanka

More than two-thirds of Sri Lankans live in rural areas far from the electricity power grid. The Practical Action charity has been helping by supplying them with small wind turbines, which people use to recharge the car batteries that power their homes.

Watering Game Reserves

In Africa, many game reserves have small wind pumps to keep waterholes filled. The pumps are similar to those still used on American farms (see page 15). A good example of wind turbine use is in Etosha National Park, in Namibia. This is one of southern Africa's most important game reserves. In

A wind turbine provides power for a small community in China's Inner Mongolia province.

One of the wind pumps that helps to water the dry regions of Namibia.

an area of 8,600 square miles (22,270 sq km), Etosha (meaning "great white place" and named after a dried-up lake) became a national park in 1907. Today, it is home to 114 species of mammals, 110 species of reptiles, and 340 species of birds. Visitors can see elephants, giraffes, rhinos, and lions. Without the wind's help in bringing water to the surface, the animals would struggle to survive in this dry environment.

Windy Patagonia

Patagonia is a dry, windswept plateau in southern Argentina. It makes up more than a quarter of Argentina but is home to less than 3 percent of the country's people. Patagonia has many remote villages and small isolated communities. Since the beginning of the twenty-first century, small wind-power projects have brought them electricity. The region has strong, constant winds, usually blowing at about 36 feet (11 m) per second (a strong breeze on the Beaufort scale), so people know they can rely on the technology. Many houses are powered by a three-blade, 39 foot (12 m) high turbine with 600 watt power.

Do Tourists Hate Wind Turbines?

Tourism is very important to many poorer countries, and it has been suggested that turbines discourage tourists. There is no real evidence to back this up, however. In Africa, wind pumps positively encourage tourism by ensuring that animals have water to drink (see above). In Denmark, where wind power is very popular, many tour companies run boat trips taking foreign visitors to see the 20 offshore wind turbines at Middelgrunden, just outside Copenhagen harbor. The turbines, which provide 4 percent of the city's electricity, have become a new landmark for tourists. In the United States, the wind farm at Searsburg, Vermont, runs successful educational tours. Their popularity has influenced locals. When the turbines were put up, two-thirds of local people supported them. After seeing their success, 83 percent of people said they felt positive about them.

Caring for the Environment

One of the greatest benefits of wind power is that it is renewable and does not harm the environment. Wind power compares favorably with nonrenewable energy sources (fossil fuels and nuclear power), and environmentalists believe that it is green and clean. Opponents claim that there are disadvantages such as noise, but most people seem to feel positive about it.

Earth's atmosphere prevents some of the Sun's rays from reaching Earth. The gases in the atmosphere also stop some heat escaping from Earth, just as glass traps warmth inside a greenhouse. We are adding to this natural greenhouse effect by emitting so many waste gases from power plants, factories, and cars. Many of these greenhouse gases—especially carbon dioxide—are produced when we burn coal, oil, or gas to release energy. Experts have discovered that this makes natural climate change more extreme. The way we use energy is adding to

The greenhouse effect traps some heat inside the atmosphere near Earth's surface. The effect is increased by carbon dioxide and other gases.

reflected

absorbed

edge of atmosphere

absorbed by atmosphere and Earth

radiation absorbed by greenhouse gases

greenhouse gases and fossil fuels

chloroflurocarbons (CFCs)

deforestation

oil and gasoline engines

Comparing Sources

Wind scores on four important counts against fossil fuels and nuclear power. As well as releasing greenhouse gases, fossil fuels pollute the atmosphere. Mining causes problems (including mining uranium for nuclear power stations), and there is no safe way to deal with nuclear waste.

Environmental problems	Wind	Nuclear	Natural gas/oil	Coal
Global warming pollution	no	no	yes	yes
Air pollution	no	no	yes	yes
Mining/extraction	no	yes	yes	yes
Disposal of waste	no	yes	no	yes

global warming, so that land, sea, and air temperatures are gradually increasing. Using renewable energy sources, such as wind, can help reduce the increase in temperature that causes global warming.

Reducing Carbon Dioxide Emissions

Carbon dioxide (CO_2) is a greenhouse gas emitted by many power sources. According to the American Wind Energy Association (AWEA), a single 1 MW wind turbine cuts the emission of CO_2 by more than 1,800 tons (1,600 t) per year compared to the normal U.S. fuel mix (including fossil fuels and nuclear power). It also cuts emissions of sulfur dioxide by 9 tons (8 t) and of nitrogen oxide by nearly 4.5 tons (4 t). Power stations would need to burn more than 1,400 tons (1,300 t) of coal or more than 1,400 barrels of oil to create the same amount of electricity.

Yes or No?

Combining surveys made over a 10-year period in Britain, the following results emerged:
• 77 percent of people are in favor of wind power;
• 14 percent are neutral (don't know);
• 9 percent are against.

How Much Energy to Build a Wind Farm?

Opponents to wind power sometimes claim that building a wind farm requires more energy than its turbines will ever generate. Experts at the British Wind Energy Association disagree. They estimate that an average wind farm should generate the amount of energy used to build it within three to five months of coming into operation. This is better than coal-fired or nuclear power stations, which take about six months—and also create problems of pollution and waste.

Noisy or Not?

One of the strongest general criticisms of wind turbines is that they are noisy. But experts say this is not the case, and long-term U.S. studies back up this view. The AWEA says, "The sound turbines produce is similar to a light whooshing or swishing sound, and much more quiet than other modern-day equipment. Even in rural or low-density areas, where there is little additional sound to mask that of the wind turbines, the sound of the blowing wind is often louder."

Other Potential Problems

Some people have suggested that wind turbines produce infrasound (low frequency noise), which cannot be heard by humans but can be felt as vibration. They are concerned that this might cause health problems for people living near wind farms, but research studies have shown that there is no cause for concern. Experts say that the infrasound levels are so low that they cannot cause any ill effects to people. However, in 2006, a family living 1,300 feet (400 m) from the nearest turbine in a 17-unit wind farm in Nova Scotia, Canada, felt forced to move because they said low frequency noise caused headaches and made them feel tired.

Shadow Flicker

This term is used to describe shadows thrown by the rotating blades of a wind turbine. Some people who live near turbines have complained about this when the sun is low in the sky. But this would only be a problem for those living very close, and it could be investigated before construction.

Land Use

One of the disadvantages of wind farms is that they require a great deal of space, although individual or small groups of turbines require much less space. Supporters point out that the space needed for a wind

An Indonesian protester hands out plants on World Environment Day (June 5) in 2007. Environmentalists promote renewable energy to help all life on Earth.

The first turbines at this wind farm at Altamont Pass, California, were put up in 1981. They have since become a well-known landmark, but they have created problems too (see page 39).

farm compares favorably with the space taken up by large hydroelectric projects with reservoirs or coal-fired power stations and the mines that supply them. Perhaps one of the biggest issues is that windswept coastlines and hills are popular with hikers and those who want to protect the environment.

Not in My Back Yard!

One of the problems with all electricity production is that people do not want to see unsightly technology from their living room window. This is known as the NIMBY (Not In My Back Yard) attitude. People are happy to have wind farms or other kinds of power stations, because they want a secure and plentiful supply of electricity, but they want them somewhere else.

According to some people, wind turbines are a blot on the landscape. But others see them as examples of modern, environmentally sound technology and find them attractive.

Modern engineers do their best to design and site wind farms so that they are not ugly. Environmental scientist James Lovelock writes: "Wind energy, through crude and unsustainable industrial development, is already devastating some unusually beautiful countryside." Greenpeace disagrees: "Compared to mountain top removal from coal mining, oil extraction, nuclear power plants, and other energy developers, wind farms are quite elegant."

What do you think? Do you like the look of wind turbines? If you do, would you want them near your home?

Danger to birds. . .

Wind turbines are a danger to birds. This is because wind farms are sited in areas where the wind blows steadily, and these locations tend to be on main routes for migratory birds. Studies have found that mice and other rodents use the bases of turbine towers as nesting places, which attracts birds of prey. As a bird circles above its prey, it is in great danger from rotating blades.

There has been a great deal of research in the United States, where it is estimated that more than 1,000 birds of prey (including 100 golden eagles) may be killed each year by turbines. Nevertheless, the American Wind Energy Association points out

Research in the United States shows that turbine blades can kill golden eagles.

Wind Energy and Wildlife

The American Wind Energy Association claims that in terms of impact on wildlife, the wind energy industry has three main benefits. It is:

• clean (environmentally friendly, protecting air quality and reducing the effects of global warming);

• compatible (with animals and humans, meaning that it does not harm them);

• committed (to ensuring minimal impact on nature and the environment).

that for every 10,000 birds killed by human activities, fewer than one is killed by a wind turbine. This single fatality compares with 5,500 deaths caused by buildings, 1,000 by domestic cats, 800 by electricity cables (some of which may be connected to wind farms), 700 by vehicles, and 700 by pesticides. In Britain, the Royal Society for the Protection of Birds says: "The available evidence suggests that appropriately positioned wind farms do not pose a significant hazard for birds. However, evidence from the U.S. and Spain confirms that poorly sited wind farms can cause severe problems for birds, through disturbance, habitat loss/damage or collision with turbines."

... and Bats

Studies have shown that bats are at risk from turbines during their autumn migration. In one year, 458 bats of seven different species were killed by 44 turbines at a West Virginia wind farm. More studies of bats are needed.

What about Offshore Farms and Fish?

Building offshore wind farms does affect marine wildlife, especially in spawning areas, and energy companies have been urged not to build during breeding periods. Turbine foundations on the seabed can act as artificial reefs and help to increase numbers of fish. However, the fishing industry is very unhappy about offshore wind farms, because they make it impossible for their boats to use these waters. Despite the conflicts, many wildlife conservationists believe that wind power should be encouraged because it combats the greatest threat of all—global warming.

Problems at Altamont Pass, California

Research has been carried out at the Altamont Pass wind farm, which has about 5,000 relatively small turbines sprawled over an area of 50 square miles (130 sq km). Recent studies suggest that as many as 1,700 to 4,700 birds may be killed there every year, including golden eagles, red-tailed hawks, American kestrels, and burrowing owls. The birds prey on the local ground squirrels. One survey found that the death rate was one bird for every five turbines per year. Environmentalists have forced the operators of the wind farm to close or move some turbines to reduce the number of birds killed. Newer turbines with a slower revolution speed also help cut the number of bird deaths.

What Does the Future Hold?

Many people see wind power as an important source of energy, and this importance is certain to grow in the future. Demand for electricity is likely to double over the next 25 years, and environmental groups will continue to put pressure on politicians and business leaders to encourage a greater use of renewable energy.

A report by the World Wind Energy Association (WWEA) states that our current use of wind power will grow by more than 25 percent in the next few years. Many countries have set high targets for the percentage of energy they will generate from renewable sources by 2020, and wind power is likely to play a large part in helping governments reach those targets. By then, experts say that 25 million U.S. homes, for example, will receive their energy from wind power.

Modern Sailing Ships

In recent years, some modern ships have added sails to reduce the amount of diesel oil and other fuels they burn when sailing conditions are good. In 2008, a new type of wind-propelled cargo ship made its maiden voyage from Germany across the Atlantic Ocean to Venezuela. This new ship has a 1,700 square foot

On its voyage across the Atlantic, the Beluga SkySails *used one-fifth less fuel than usual by also using wind power. This has caught the attention of other shipping companies.*

40

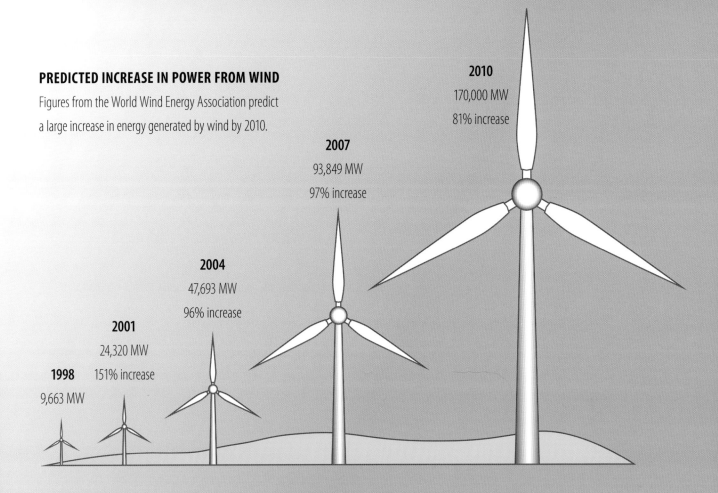

PREDICTED INCREASE IN POWER FROM WIND

Figures from the World Wind Energy Association predict a large increase in energy generated by wind by 2010.

2010
170,000 MW
81% increase

2007
93,849 MW
97% increase

2004
47,693 MW
96% increase

2001
24,320 MW
151% increase

1998
9,663 MW

(160 sq m) kite-sail, similar to the sail of a paraglider, which flies up to 1,000 feet (300 m) above the ship and allows high-level winds to tow it along. The operators of the cargo ship believe that the sail will save up to 35 percent of the ship's fuel. It will also lower harmful carbon emissions.

Floating Turbines

Researchers at the Massachusetts Institute of Technology (MIT) and the U.S. National Renewable Energy Laboratory (NREL) have designed a wind turbine that can be attached to a floating platform. Steel cables secure the platform to a mooring on the ocean floor. Tests have shown that the floating platforms could survive hurricane winds. They could operate in much deeper water than current offshore turbines and further out to sea.

Counting the Cost

Experts claim that the cost of wind-generated electricity has fallen dramatically. Wind power capacity has doubled every three years, and prices have fallen each time by 15 percent. Wind energy now competes with new coal and nuclear power, even before environmental costs are taken into account. Wind associations believe that the price of wind-generated electricity will continue to fall. This depends on investment and incentives (see page 23). The AWEA says: "There are no fuel costs, and in good locations the 'levelized' cost (the capital, the fuel, and the operations and maintenance costs over the lifetime of the plant) of wind energy can now be very competitive with that of other energy sources." Wind power costs are fixed and predictable.

Dividing Communities

The issue of large wind farms divides opinion all over the world. One example of the division of public attitudes is a proposal to build a 181-turbine wind farm on the Isle of Lewis, off the coast of western Scotland. The farm could produce 600 MW of electricity—enough to supply all the homes in Glasgow (Scotland's largest city). But it is an enormous project requiring 137 large pylons to carry 19 miles (31 km) of overhead electricity cables, as well as the construction of 88 miles (142 km) of access roads. The project would create an enormous number of jobs and offer a huge income to the people of Lewis. Though some islanders are convinced of the advantages, many are not and continue to protest against the wind farm. There are likely to be more debates in the future.

Wind-Powered Buildings?

In the future, it may prove possible to include wind turbines in tall buildings. Architects and designers are planning to build large rotors into skyscrapers or perhaps on top of the buildings. One problem is that buildings in cities cause turbulence, so that the wind streams are not constant or steady. Also, the proposed rotors take up a great deal of space. Nevertheless, it may be possible for a tall building to generate its own electricity for residents or workers.

Airborne Ideas

Scientists, engineers, and inventors constantly work on new ideas for harvesting the wind. Many are concentrating on reaching high-speed winds higher in the sky. Some scientists in the Netherlands are working on a system called a laddermill that has a loop of kites that rotate in the wind and turn a cable. An Australian professor is developing another system—the gyromill. This would fly up to 2.8 miles (4.5 km) above the ground and send back electricity generated by spinning rotors.

This is how the wind-power system called a gyromill might look. It is just one of the exciting new developments in wind power being tested.

Will the Wind Debate Continue?

People will continue to debate the merits of wind power, regardless of how successfully it increases its share of electricity production. Some believe that wind will never produce enough power to be taken seriously. Others believe that all renewable energy sources must be explored and invested in to combat global warming. People are divided on the environmental effects of wind turbines in open landscapes. Many believe that wind farms are essential and should be accommodated in the best way possible; others disagree. The arguments for both sides will help you to make up your mind.

Fluttering Power

Closer to the ground, American inventors are working on using the "aeroelastic flutter" or vibration caused by moving air to power microwind devices. They work by allowing a vibrating membrane to drive a minigenerator.

Glossary

anemometer A device that measures wind speed.

carbon dioxide (CO$_2$) A greenhouse gas given off when fossil fuels are burned.

carbon fiber A strong, light, synthetic material.

circulation Free movement in a circular direction.

circumference The distance around the boundary of a circle or sphere.

climate change A change in general weather conditions over a long period of time, including temperature changes, more or less rain, droughts, etc.

clipper A fast sailing ship with tall masts and many sails.

cogwheel A toothed wheel that fits together with another wheel to turn it.

continental shelf The sloping underwater area near land at the edge of a continent.

deflect To change the course of something.

drag Resistance when moving through air.

dike An embankment built to hold back water and stop flooding.

dynamo A machine that turns mechanical energy into electrical energy.

electricity grid A large network of cables for transmitting electrical power.

generator A machine that turns mechanical energy into electrical energy.

glass fiber Strong thread made by pulling molten glass through a narrow opening.

global warming Heating up of Earth's surface, especially caused by pollution from burning fossil fuels.

greenhouse effect Warming of Earth's surface, especially caused by pollution from burning fossil fuels.

housing A covering that protects machine parts.

hub The central part of a rotor.

incandescent Producing light from great heat.

knot A unit for measuring speed (1 knot = 1.15 mile (1.85 km) per hour).

meteorologist A scientist who studies the weather.

nitrogen oxide A colorless, poisonous gas.

nonrenewable energy Energy that is used up and cannot be replaced (from sources such as coal, gas, oil, or uranium).

patent A document giving an inventor the exclusive right to make, use, or sell something.

polder An area of land drained and reclaimed from the sea.

prefabricate   To make something in sections in a factory, ready to be assembled somewhere else.

prevailing wind   The most common wind direction in a particular place.

renewable energy or resources   Sources of energy that do not run out such as biomass, geothermal, solar, water, and wind power.

rotation   Turning motion; spinning.

rotor   The spinning assembly and blades of a turbine.

sulfur dioxide (SO_2)   A poisonous gas given off by burning coal.

tariff   A fee; price charged.

trade wind   A tropical wind blowing toward the equator from the east.

turbine   A machine with rotating blades that turn a shaft.

turbulence   Gusty movements of air.

wind farm or park   A large number of wind turbines in one area.

windshaft   The shaft or pole to which the sails of a windmill are attached.

Web Sites

The World Wind Energy Association
www.world-wind-energy.info

Global Wind Energy Council
www.gwec.net

The Danish Wind Industry Association (with a Guided Tour on Wind Energy)
www.windpower.org/en/tour.htm

American Wind Energy Association (with a Small Wind section)
www.awea.org/smallwind

Wind Farms of the World
www.ilr.tu-berlin.de/WKA/windfarm.html

UK Sustainable Development Commission
www.sd-commission.org.uk/pages/wind.html

Index